Choose 2
Think

Pickleball Passion

A Marriage Devotional

21-Days to Stronger Connection

on and off the Court

by

VICTORIA D. LYDON

First edition.

The author is grateful for permission to include these copyrighted materials:

All Scripture quotations, unless otherwise indicated, are taken from the Holy Bible, New International Version®, NIV®. Copyright ©1973, 1978, 1984, 2011 by Biblica, Inc.® Used by permission of Zondervan. All rights
reserved worldwide. www.zondervan.com The "NIV" and "New International Version" are trademarks registered
in the United States Patent and Trademark Office by Biblica, Inc.®

Wings of Dawn Ministries, LLC
www.choose2think.co
417 Meadow Valley Rd.
Lexington, KY 40511

For discounted, bulk orders over 25 copies, please contact Victoria at choose2think@gmail.com.

Thank you for purchasing this book!

HERE'S YOUR FREE GIFT

50 Take-Action Items to Rev up Your Marriage (includes ideas for conversations and date nights as well as other practical applications designed to help you stay connected and build deeper intimacy)

Visit: www.choose2think.co **and click PICKLEBALL FREEBIE**

ALSO BY THE AUTHOR

*Choose 2 Think: Find Peace, Joy, Hope, Health &
Freedom Every Day! 365 Daily Devotions*

*Choose 2 Think: Find Peace, Joy, Hope, Health &
Freedom Every Day! Journal*

WITH DEEPEST GRATITUDE TO GOD,
MY FAMILY, AND
ALL OUR PICKLEBALL PLAYING FRIENDS

DEDICATION

To Jim, my Gem

HEARTFELT THANKS

To Sara A. Morgan

FORWARD

Meet Victoria and Jim

On a scorching hot and sunny day in June, Jim and I married on the front porch of my parents' house in Winchester, KY. Our ceremony was informal and simple (the way I like it!) and topped off with a BBQ lunch.

All our six children and their spouses, our grandchildren, and parents, plus my sister (she is a saint--she did sooo much to help that day!) and my nephew graced us with their treasured presence.

We invited guests to wear shorts and T-shirts - nothing fancy. No gifts, no fanfare, just their lovely faces.

My two sweet granddaughters, each carrying a small bouquet of white daisies, kicked off the event by slowly walking along the front sidewalk to one of the most beautiful wedding songs I've ever heard in my life called "I Choose You" by Ryann Darling.

You must promise to listen to the entire song because it's really about God's amazing love for Y O U.

Of course, when Jim and I walked down the sidewalk a few moments later, I bawled.

I mean think about it.

Nearly 20 years single, yet God's amazing mercy and provision had blessed my family every moment. After 19 years of homeschooling, my four kids were now "launched," finished with college, married, and starting their own families.

And then this godly man enters my life? Indeed. And it was time, the dawning of a new and exciting season....

I met Jim, my dog-loving, laundry-doing, belly-laughing, amazingly humble and intelligent 5-star hubby, in the summer of 2019 playing tennis through Frankfort Parks and Rec. We later switched to pickleball, and that's really where our love story began. Yes, pickleball is not only the best sport ever, as you might also agree, it is a great way to meet people, especially future spouses!

After months of struggling to figure out how to get to know each other--and believe me, Jim had to work very hard because I was clueless and quite reticent--finally God gave me the courage to take this huge step toward the possibility of remarriage. There was much at stake as we would attempt to merge 11 adult children as well as our folks into a brand-new extended family.

During our slow-mo-get-to-know phase, we created a few terms to help us define our budding relationship.

Like "fraquaintances" = a guy and gal who are more than acquaintances but not yet friends (there are many boundaries for this type of relationship); and "non-dating" = what a faith-filled couple in their 50s say they're doing when they don't know what they're doing (it's really dating, but a whole lot less serious, sorta) and again a ton of boundaries here.

Needless to say, after about three months of non-dating, we actually made it official around Thanksgiving of 2021, got engaged in early May of 2022, and were married about two months later. When you know, you know. I really did get my gold medal, all right. Let me be the first to say, "Praise be to God from whom all blessings flow."

These days we cozy down in our home in Lexington. I continue to teach online college Spanish classes from home, and Jim works for the state.

You may be wondering how the thought of writing a devotional about pickleball ever came about. In a nutshell, after a couple of years playing ball with my husband, I discovered that my heart suffered from disordered love (an Augustinian phrase): I loved winning more than God at times and consequently more than my husband in many ways! I know. This sounds absurd!

Long story short: I knew that if my husband and I could face and beat the emotional "giants" we faced on the pickleball court, our marriage would be infinitely stronger. We would keep Jesus on the throne of our hearts. In other words, playing pickleball together revealed to me many unwholesome and ungodly attitudes housed in my Christ-loving heart, and something had to go.

My hope is that you will find yourself somewhere in the pages of this devotional. I know you enjoy pickleball and that you likely are married. And if you are like the many pickleball loving married couples that I know, you, too, long to play ball properly with your spouse and enjoy the game with them! This devotional will help you get the ball flying, so to speak, spark lots of conversation topics for you, and by God's grace, give you the courage to continue to foster and grow one of your most valuable human relationships on earth: your marriage.

This sounds easy, but we have learned that it requires a lot of effort and intention. Just recently Jim and I did our annual marriage tune-up (you can find the tune-up at the end of this book), and this experience was quite telling.

As I gazed across the table into his eyes, my heart melted with love for him. Number one: he had the courage to do the tune-up with me! Number two: he bravely answered all the questions honestly and with pointed transparency. Number three: I learned something I didn't know about us, something that gave me an opportunity to grow and gave him a chance to watch the change in me.

By the end of the evening my belly was filled with a grilled black bean sandwich and fries, and my heart was filled with sheer gratitude to God for blessing me and my family with this amazing man.

What you hold in your hands or view electronically is a powerhouse of encouragement to improve your relationship with your spouse. It is a fuel box of fun waiting to be lit. Make these next three weeks an adventure for you, much like climbing a high mountain or trekking through unknown territory. Enjoy one another. Laugh. Keep things simple. Pray and play together. Allow God to probe your heart and mind. Choose your thoughts wisely, those thoughts that testify of who God is, what He says about you and Himself. Invest in one another. You will reap huge rewards!

Remember, in addition to the tune-up, please take advantage of the freebie that comes with this book and contains over 50 take-action items that make extra-special date nights and conversation starters with your spouse.

Visit www.choose2think.co and click PICKLEBALL FREEBIE to download or print your free resource!

Love,

Victoria

PS: If you're ever in Lexington, reach out! Maybe Jim and I can take on you and your spouse in a fun game of pickleball. We'll meet you on the courts!

When I have learned to love God better
than my earthly dearest, I shall love
my earthly dearest better than I do now.

– *C.S. Lewis*

DAY 1: The Best Team Ever - Communication Is Key

Two are better than one because they have a good return for their labor: If either of them falls down, one can help the other up. But pity anyone who falls and has no one to help them up. (Ecclesiastes 4:9-10)

Teamwork and communication go together in marriage and on the pickleball court. Ever have a shot to the center fall right between you and your partner? You look at each other as if to say, "That was yours." Or how about this: The shot comes center and both you and your spouse go for the ball smacking paddles and sending the ball sailing out of bounds? The forehand player smugly looks at their spouse and quips, "Forehand takes the center!"

Just as the simple act of calling "yours" or "mine" divides good players from great players, communicating with your spouse clearly and openly divides good marriages from great ones. Open, honest lines of communication keep you united and strong as a team, which leads to a happier and more fulfilling marriage on and off the court.

Jim tells me that I sigh and shrug my shoulders a lot when he misses a ball or makes an unforced error; I've caught him rolling his eyes when I make mistakes or get frustrated (which frustrates him!). Truly your body language communicates far more than words. Your countenance speaks volumes. Avoid frowning, knitting your brows, or clenching your teeth. Choose grace to help you reorient your negative or critical thoughts and attitudes.

Watch your timing, too. Once, during tournament play, Jim scolded me for continuing to hit balls that were flying out. "You're already in your head, Victoria. I can tell!" he firmly noted. My feathers weren't just ruffled at that moment, they were in full peacock mode. I imploded. We lost the game.

Later, I said, "Gee, do you mind not critiquing me when we are playing? I need to know what I'm doing wrong, and I want to correct my mistakes, but if you say something during game play, we might as well forfeit." We both agreed that effective communication not only requires using uplifting speech and posture, but it also needs the proper timing.

On the court and in your marriage, when you are cooperative and demonstrate teamwork and unity, your brain stimulates the release of oxytocin, the "love" hormone. This powerhouse hormone strengthens the emotional bond and deepens the connections you have with your spouse. Divisiveness and criticism have the opposite effect.

Nearly every day, Jim and I fondly say of one another, "We are the best team ever!" When I text him, I type in *#bestteamever*. What you focus on grows. Do you sincerely want to be a better team with your spouse? Think you are one, and your brain will prove you right!

Give your spouse the benefit of the doubt. They are probably trying their hardest on and off the court. They are learning like you are. You both bring your distinct qualities to your relationship. Embrace your roles as a team, supporting and uplifting each other, knowing that together, you can face and conquer any challenge that comes your way. You can also change and grow as children of the Most High God. He is in the heart transformation business, after all!

Reflection: In what ways do you and your spouse make an amazing team? Where would you both most like to improve when it comes to better communication?

Prayer: Dear God, thank you for bringing us together in life. Help us to remember that You are the core and strength of our marriage. May we learn to communicate clearly and support each other, both on and off the court. Amen.

We are here to love. Not much else matters.

—*Francis Chan*

DAY 2: Serving with Intention

You, my brothers and sisters, were called to be free. But do not use your freedom to indulge the flesh, rather, serve one another humbly in love. (Galatians 5:13).

In pickleball, a successful serve requires concentration and determination. "Zero, zero, two," or "Zero, zero, start," marks your first opportunity to begin the game with the potential to score. Similarly, in your marriage, you must be deliberate about committing your ways to God and trusting in His guidance as your starting point every single day. You serve God first, then your family, your church, and community.

A steady serve requires muscle memory and keen focus. During high stakes moments, avoid the margins—instead, simply "put the ball in the box." In marriage, you may be faced with untold challenges, but if you consistently put the "ball" in the box of trusting, supporting, and serving one another, your brain rewires, fostering emotional security and deeper intimacy.

Once Jim and I battled hard in what appeared to be a come-back streak. Our opponents had us 9-3. We inched up two points during our serve, then held them to nine. On the next side-out, we inched up a few more points, put forth our best defensive strategy, then held them to nine again. Our serve. We took another point. Their serve. Hold. We were gaining. It's now 8 serving 9. My serve. In a split-second attempt to hit deep, the ball sailed out of bounds narrowly missing the base line. Jim's turn, and you need to know that if Jim is speaking when he serves, well, it's almost always less than favorable. He half smiled and mumbled to me, "It's okay, just play this ball." Without a pause, he relayed the score and served – directly into the net.

Momentum drained out of our souls as we looked at one another with bewilderment and disappointment. "No worries," he chimed. Yet that double fault was just the break our opponents needed. We did not give up, but the tide had turned in their favor, and they clinched the win.

When you step to the line to serve, your single task is to put the ball over the net and into play. If you find yourself nervous before serving, especially when the stakes are high, practice deep breathing and visualization techniques. Visualize that solid serve to increase your confidence. Take your time and tune out the noises around you. Make sure your partner is in the proper position. Did you know that after you call the score, you have ten seconds to serve?

As you take the serve, whisper to yourself thoughts like: *Put the ball in the box. Deep breath. You can do this. Focus. You've done this before, now do it again.*

Just as a steady serve sets the tone for the game, the love you show sets the tone for your marriage. Try expressing your love and appreciation to your spouse consistently. Serve up kindness, patience, and affection daily on and off the court, and your marriage will flourish.

Reflection: For you, what is the hardest element of serving (in a pickleball game and in life)? How do you demonstrate love, commitment, and trust toward God and your spouse?

Prayer: Heavenly Father, help us remain committed to you. Thank you for loving us whether we wildly or narrowly miss your heart. Help us to be gracious and encouraging with one another when we blow our serves. Teach us to rely fully on you as we serve one another. May we learn from our mistakes and always serve up our best shot. Amen.

To love means loving the unlovable.
To forgive means pardoning the unpardonable.
Faith means believing the unbelievable.
Hope means hoping when everything seems hopeless.

–Generally attributed to G.K. Chesterton

DAY 3: The Pickleball Drive - Go All In

Do everything in love. (1 Corinthians 16:14)

To drive or drop is often a split-second decision in the game. The beauty of a powerful drive shot is that it can keep your opponents back at the base line or it can catch them off guard at the net. Who doesn't love those marginal drives that fly down the sidelines and kiss the edge of the line?

Your opponent's backhand and the center court are the best targets for your drives. When should you drive? Try driving the ball when your opponents hit a short or lofty serve return, on your third shot (instead of a drop), or as a speed-up tactic. Strike the ball with passion and determination but be mindful not to overdo your swing and force.

When you go all-in with your pickleball drive, you give it your best shot, focusing on technique, power, and placement. The intensity of this type of return releases adrenaline and boosts your focus and energy.

Jim and I both played tennis prior to playing pickleball, and you can easily tell by watching how we drive the ball. We swing fast and follow through, striking the ball like lightning into our opponents' court. I cannot recount the times Jim delivered a low drive past our rivals though they stood ready and waiting at the net. His accuracy and intention mattered.

It's the same in marriage. When you pour your heart into everything you do, always acting in love, you'll find God's Spirit behind those big gestures and His gentle whisper behind the precision with the little things. Maybe you plan a huge surprise party for your spouse or an intimate weekend getaway or a simple date night in your living room after the kids are in bed.

In all scenarios, you fully and deliberately invest time, effort, and emotions into your marriage. Just as the pickleball drive requires your full commitment to the shot, your marriage flourishes when you both are fully dedicated to making it work.

Reflection: In what pickleball scenarios are drives powerfully important? What can you do this week to deepen your relationship with your spouse, showing them that you are all in?

Prayer: Heavenly Father, fill us with your love so that it overflows into everything we do. May our actions, both on the pickleball court and in our marriage, be driven by our extraordinary love for one another. Amen.

Marriage is a call to die [to self]... Christian marriage vows are the inception of a lifelong practice of death, of giving over not only all you have, but all you are. Is this a grim gallows call? Not at all! It is no more grim than dying to self and following Christ. In fact, those who lovingly die for their [spouses] are those who know the most joy, have the most fulfilling marriages, and experience the most love.

– R. Kent Hughes

DAY 4: The Third Shot Drop - A Delicate Balance

Live in harmony with one another. Do not be proud, but be willing to associate with people of low position. Do not be conceited. (Romans 12:16)

The third shot drop has quite a few advantages: it helps to slow the game down and may allow you and your partner to get to the net. Dropping a shot into your opponents' non-volley zone (NVZ) or kitchen area can balance out otherwise hard-hitting play. In your marriage, seeking harmony by meeting your spouse's needs to the best of your ability goes a long way. When you slow things down to focus on your partner's thoughts and contributions to your marriage, you make room for appreciation and joy to surface in your otherwise fast-moving life.

Your drop needs to be low and land in the NVZ because if your drop is a bit too high and lofty, it can be detrimental and queue up the ball for your opponent to quickly slam it back to your side in a sudden put-away.

Just as drilling the drop improves your pickleball game, repeatedly practicing humility and self-sacrifice with your spouse adds polish to your marriage. You both aim to communicate assertively, express your needs and desires respectfully, and find ways to bring peace and harmony into each day, which all lead to deep satisfaction and mutual contentment.

Executing a drop shot in pickleball requires a gentle touch and a well-timed release. The player who watches their partner strike the ball must carefully follow their lead to stay back at the baseline or move to the net.

I cannot tell you the times I have, at the last minute, decided to drive the ball instead of drop it. I try to go center, but instead my drive goes right to the net player which essentially makes Jim a sitting duck as he is standing near our side of the net waiting for my drop. I have also attempted the drop with Jim positioned at the net only to loft the ball a bit too high which makes Jim recoil with his paddle down in an attempt to defend our opponent's powerful, lightning-fast slam to his knees.

Unfortunately, when your drop is attackable you feed your partner to the sharks on a silver platter. After my misplaced shots, he glances at me as if to say, "Victoria, keep the drop low." Sometimes he laughs when he sees my sheepish, half grin. I beat him with the reminder to drop the ball just over the net. Fortunately, Jim graciously realizes it's easier said than done.

Maintaining a delicate balance in your pickleball partnership involves understanding each other's strengths and weaknesses, adapting your strategy, and supporting each other's growth. You can embrace the art of balancing on the court and in your marriage to create a lasting, harmonious connection where there is no room for prideful or conceited play. You recognize you are both trying your hardest and doing your very best.

Reflection: Does your marriage feel "balanced" to you and your spouse? Are there any areas that need to be addressed? What can you do to keep the focus on your marriage aligned with your overall life goals?

Prayer: Dear God, help us to live in harmony with one another as a team. May we be humble and considerate, valuing each other's uniqueness and treating one another with respect. Show us how to keep our daily actions aligned with our values. Amen.

Jesus' teaching in general [implies] that happy and fulfilling sexual relations in marriage depend on each partner aiming to give satisfaction to the other. If it is the joy of each to make the other happy, a hundred problems will be solved before they happen.

– John Piper

DAY 5: The Pickleball Dink - A Call to Patiently Endure

Let us not grow weary of doing good, for in due season we will reap if we do not give up. (Galatians 6:9)

The delicate and deliberate dink shot in pickleball not only requires finesse, but it also demands great patience. Likewise, in your marriage, patience is the golden ticket to change and growth. Growth is hard to see, isn't it? But if you don't give up, by God's grace, you will see the rewards of your hard work!

Once, Jim and I left the court, and for the first time in a long while [sigh], I wasn't pouty or terribly disgruntled. "How about that, Jim?" I declared with glee. "I'm getting better! I'm really changing! All these prayers and petitions to remove my dratted competitive spirit are finally being answered!"

"I see that," he answered, rising to my level of enthusiasm. We even lost several games, and you didn't get in your head."

Sometimes transformation is a slow burn, just like dinking. You dink. They dink. You dink. They dink. You slightly change your dink. They slightly change their dink. You put a little spin on your dink. They dink the return. You angle deeply to get them off the court, yet they dink back with equal angle. You dink short to center. They dink short to center. And so it goes...until that fatal moment when the dink is attackable! Smash! You win the point! And let's just say, there is nothing in pickleball quite like attacking your opponent's attackable dink because not only did you show finesse and focus, but you also patiently waited!

Tactically, dinking is the set-up for winning plays. Being patient in your marriage is much the same. Patience is referred to as long suffering, and it's a fruit of the Spirit and a backbone characteristic of love.

Demonstrating patience in your marriage is like dancing in sync with your partner. Back when Jim and I were dating, we decided to try dance classes that he had bought through an online app. Night after night, I followed his lead. Sometimes I goofed, stepped on his toes, or missed the step choreography.

Dinking in pickleball relies on soft touches and a certain gentleness that goes with patience. Similarly, in your marriage, practicing patience with one another allows you to approach conflicts with grace and understanding, fostering a spirit of compromise and growth.

Reflection: On a scale of 1-10 how would you rank the patience of yourself and your spouse (10 being the highest degree)? Compare your answers with your spouse and explain why. What areas of your marriage require the most patience now? Have you seen any personal growth in this area lately?

Prayer: Dear God, help us to cultivate patience in our hearts and actions. May we seek to serve one another in love and put each other's needs before our own. Just as You suffered, help us to endure all difficulties we may face for the joy before us. Amen.

Marriage was ordained for a remedy and
to increase the world and for the man to help the woman
and the woman the man,
with all love and kindness.

--*William Tyndale*

DAY 6: The Pickleball Volley - Respond with Love

Dear friends, let us love one another, for love comes from God. Everyone who loves has been born of God and knows God. Whoever does not love does not know God, because God is love. (1 John 4:7-8)

In pickleball, quick reflexes and coordination are essential for successful volleys. Similarly, in your marriage, you can choose to respond to each other with love and grace, knowing that love first comes from God and is the foundation of your relationship.

When Jim is at the kitchen line, I often stand in awe of his Herculean reflexes and fast hits. My hands are fast, but somehow, he has an incredible knack at responding quickly. His lightning-fast reflexes and coordination amaze me. Sometimes as his partner, I feel so relieved when those heated volleys never touch my paddle!

Responding with love in marriage ought to be just as fast! When you remember that Jesus Christ was the first responder in your life, the one who brought you from death to life, the one who demonstrated His great love for you by taking all the hard shots to your heart, and the one who placed the weight of your sin upon His shoulders, then you, too, may stand in awe of His mercy, goodness, and love.

Sometimes in volleys, Jim and I both may fall short. Yet what better way to acknowledge our shortcomings, offer forgiveness and grace to one another, and then try again. Cultivating a culture of grace and understanding on the court takes time and requires attention. Just as in marriage, you must remind yourself that mistakes are a part of the game. They are not deal breakers, but rather avenues to deeper trust and resilience. Be quick to encourage your partner when they make a mistake.

One way you can respond with love in your marriage is to become an apt listener. Attentive listening communicates love and support and can alleviate stress and strengthen emotional intimacy. Respond to every "volley" with love, and your marriage will thrive with deeper connection.

Reflection: What issues of life seem to be coming hard at you and your spouse these days? How do you respond as a team?

Prayer: Heavenly Father, teach us to love one another as you have loved us. May our responses to each other be filled with love, kindness, and understanding. Amen.

Men, you'll never be a good groom to your wife
unless you're first a good bride to Jesus.

--Dr. Timothy Keller

DAY 7: The Pickleball Rally - Perseverance in Unity

...then make my joy complete by being like-minded, having the same love, being one in spirit and of one mind. (Philippians 2:2)

According to the *Guinness Book of World Records*, "The longest pickleball rally is 16,046 and was achieved by Angelo A. Rossetti and Ettore Rosetti (both USA) in Rocky Hill, Connecticut, USA, on 10 October 2021 (Guinessworldrecords.com). Can you even imagine?

I bet you can think of a few long or heated rallies between the pros that you have enjoyed watching. Maybe you and your spouse have participated in exciting, even nail-biting rallies. What is the secret to long-lasting rallies? In addition to patience and focus, I'd like to suggest a concept called "shadowing."

Shadowing in pickleball is when you and your partner move together on the court as if your feet were connected by an invisible rope. Your spouse goes left; you go left. Your spouse stays at the baseline; you stay at the baseline. Your spouse runs off court to snatch a return, you move with them in that direction. You play in each other's shadow in tandem and unity.

Isn't this also true of marriage? You love one another in truth and spirit in whichever direction the other goes. You support each other through every challenge and trial. You stand, you pause, you pray, and you advance together as a team.

Pickleball rallies require mental and physical endurance and resilience. You must move yet stay present in the moment making each shot count. Often you will avoid making risky shots especially when a match point is at stake.

The pickleball rally reflects the ups and downs of life and the discretionary movement you must make together in life and marriage. As you and your spouse confront challenges together, you can persevere as a team, stand united in purpose, and remain unwavering in your support for one another.

What's more, when you and your spouse are besieged with trials and face untold challenges in your life, there is another one to whom you can choose to stay extremely close, the One who leads you and cares most for you: your Heavenly Father. You can hide and find refuge in the shadow of His wings. The psalmist writes: "Because you are my help, I sing in the shadow of your wings" (Psalm 63:7). When God moves, you follow. When God stays put, you stop. When God nudges you to the left or right, you obey His voice.

Reflection: In what ways are you and your spouse united in marriage? How do you present yourself as you face each day: as a team, moving in tandem or a bit distanced and separated?

Prayer: Lord, too often, one of us goes rogue and tries to handle things on our own. Help us instead to depend on you and to be united in our hearts and minds. Strengthen our behavior as a team and grant us the perseverance to overcome any obstacles that come our way. May we remember that we do life with You and in Your shadow. Amen.

Success in marriage is more than finding the right person: it is being the right person.

--Robert Browning

DAY 8: The Pickleball Drop Shot - Gentle and Kind

A gentle answer turns away wrath, but a harsh word stirs up anger. (Proverbs 15:1)

Here's the scenario: From the odd serving side, you place a hard serve into your opponents' court. With equal force, they drive the ball back to you deep in your court. You bend your knees and gently strike the ball, removing its speed and dropping it in the right corner of the non-volley zone (NVZ) or "kitchen" on your opponents' side. The opposing player must now make a backhand hit to keep the ball in play. They scoop it a bit too high, and your partner forcefully delivers the slam shot to score the point.

Drop shots require finesse and a whole lot of practice. Executing them strategically during match play helps you to outmaneuver your opponents and ultimately builds confidence in your game.

In pickleball, the drop shot requires a gentle touch. Similarly, in your marriage, there are times when you will want to return a hard blow with kindness, compassion, and forgiveness. Instead of barking back, you choose to quickly let go of grudges and show grace to your spouse. Like placing a soft drop shot just over the net, your tender words and actions can defuse tense situations and create increased harmony in your marriage.

Being gentle and kind with each other during a disagreement gives each partner time to pause and respond instead of harshly react. This behavior strengthens emotional intimacy between you both.

In your marriage, you may think it's not fair that you must be the one who is gentle and kind. You may grow weary in consistently returning a soft answer during heated exchanges. Brain science supports the notion that the more you model this type of interpersonal skill, the more your spouse will learn through simple observation alone.

Lay down your pride and keep choosing to engage and promote gentleness, kindness, and self-control. After all, these are traits of the Holy Spirit within you. Allow the Spirit to move through you in your marriage to create a loving and nurturing relationship.

Reflection: How comfortable do you feel with your drop shots? Can you commit to drilling and practicing these shots weekly until you improve your technique? In marriage, which partner seems gentler and kinder? Which one defuses arguments instead of adding fuel to the fire? What can you both learn?

Prayer: Dear God, teach us to be gentle and kind with each other. Grant us the ability to forgive as You have forgiven us. May our love and marriage be characterized by compassion and understanding. Help us to be quick to listen but slow to speak. Amen.

A happy marriage is the union of two good forgivers.

—Widely attributed to Ruth Graham

Day 9: The Pickleball Lob - Aim High!

Set your minds on things above, not on earthly things. (Colossians 3:2)

Ever face off with two fierce opponents at the net who seem to be backboards for every shot you pound their way? If so, there's nothing quite so effective at getting them off the net than a well-placed lob shot. An offensive lofted shot may catch your opponent off guard, forcing them back to the baseline and allowing your team to take control of the net.

When I make a lob, sometimes I consider it a bit scrappy, especially when the sun is overhead, and my opponents just might be a bit blinded. I really love to lob when those taller players loom at the net–it's an opportunity to push them to the baseline so that Jim and I can move forward and take control of the net. Jim, on the other hand, doesn't lob as much, but he occasionally gently scoops the ball over our opponents when we are all dinking. Lobbing is a strategic, necessary shot in the game.

Lobbing sends the focus upward for all players, and an upward focus in your marriage is critical. In other words, keeping your spiritual eyes aimed toward God, seeing the bigger picture, seeking God's guidance, and setting your mind on heavenly principles will strengthen your relationship and help you to regain control when faced with roadblocks or "giants."

Aiming high in marriage not only means you're fixated on the "Author and Perfecter of your faith," it may also mean you're dreaming together. Just as you aim your lob shot high over your opponents, let your shared aspirations soar beyond the ordinary. Pursue God's purpose for your marriage with enthusiasm, faith, and anticipation for the great adventures that await you.

Reflection: What are the pros and cons of lobbing the ball in pickleball? How does keeping your eyes on God strengthen your marriage and draw you individually closer to Him?

Prayer: Heavenly Father, help us to fix our eyes on You and Your ways. May our hearts and minds be aligned with Your will as we seek to grow together in love and understanding. May we never stop dreaming and may Your will be done in our lives! Amen.

A Christian marriage is [not] one with no problems or even a
marriage with fewer problems. (It may well mean more problems.)
But it does mean a life in which two people may become
more able to accept each other and love each other in the midst
of problems and fears. It means a marriage in which selfish people
can sometimes accept selfish people without constantly
trying to change them—and even accept themselves, because
they realize personally that they have been accepted by Christ.

—*Keith Miller*

DAY 10: The Pickleball Slam - Handling Conflict

"In your anger, do not sin: Do not let the sun go down while you are still angry, and do not give the devil a foothold" [Jesus]. (Ephesians 4:26-27)

The powerful slam in pickleball can be exciting but should be controlled. Likewise, in your marriage, you may feel slammed at times. How will you handle harsh reactions or words that come your way? How will you deliver your anger in healthy, God-honoring fashion without letting frustrations, dissatisfactions, or annoyances fester. Try to address issues promptly, seeking resolution in love.

When I strike an overhead shot, slamming it back to my opponents, I must be controlled and precise in my swing and placement. Admittedly, when I miss the slam, I am inwardly kicking myself for not placing the shot in a better spot, i.e., the center of my opponents' court for starters. Sometimes I'm so tempted to go to the margins with the slam because it is a likelier put away. Sadly, I've dished out my share of verbal slams to Jim while playing, only to feel ashamed and disgruntled at my lack of self-control and God-honoring speech.

On one occasion, I missed three shots in a row, aka unforced errors. Jim, a solid and consistent player, happens to shoot a line drive that lands out of play, and I quickly reprimand him, "For crying out loud, Jim! Go center!" My verbal slam was a hit to his heart and ego, and I recoiled in dismay with myself, and maybe [just saying] our disrespectful communication was a catalyst to losing that game.

Defensively receiving a slammed ball can be equally challenging, testing your grit, tenacity, and patience. Sometimes you may not be able to do anything except get your paddle down and hope for the best. It feels the same way in marriage especially when you are on the receiving end of a heated exchange laced with a slam or two. Whether dishing out a damaging slam or being on the receiving end of one, God's message is clear: don't give the enemy a foothold.

When Jim and I prioritize open and respectful communication with one another, addressing concerns calmly and constructively, our "slams" are targeted and foster a supportive and encouraging atmosphere. When we receive a harsh word with compassion, attempting to validate the other's feelings instead of stirring up drama, we are Christ-like.

The pickleball slam is a powerful shot that requires control and precision to avoid errors. Similarly, handling conflict with your spouse involves expressing your thoughts and feelings respectfully, avoiding harsh words or emotional outbursts. You both can improve your communication methods and conflict resolution strategies so your marriage will flourish and become stronger and healthier.

Reflection: How do you and your spouse handle conflict on and off the court? Do either of you tend to be the "peace maker"? How is conflict management an opportunity to glorify the Lord?

Prayer: Heavenly Father, grant us wisdom and self-control when dealing with conflicts. May we always seek resolution with love and understanding, not giving room for resentment or bitterness. Amen.

A successful marriage requires falling in love many times, always with the same person.

--*Mignon McLaughlin*

DAY 11: Pickleball Power - Deference is Key

Wives, submit yourselves to your own husbands as you do to the Lord. For the husband is the head of the wife as Christ is the head of the church, his body, of which he is the Savior. (Ephesians 5:22-23)

As you know, I love overhead smashes. When they come my way, a shot of adrenaline bursts through my body. I am split-second giddy with anticipation. Just as I raise my left hand to follow the ball and bend my right elbow poised to strike, I hear Jim say, "Mine." Quickly, I try to move aside, giving him room to put the ball away. Once, however, I called the ball and he didn't, so I proceeded to make my smashing move. I heard his feet shuffling slightly behind me and I caught sight of his shadow. The next thing I knew, we crashed, sending me sideways on my right knee to the concrete with him virtually on top of me and the ball bouncing in our court.

Later he reminded me, "You've got to let me have the overheads, Victoria, especially when they are on my forehand side." To him, this ought to be the norm and rightly so. He is much stronger than I am. He puts the ball away, whereas if I don't angle an attempted put away, my shots are aptly returned by our rivals. Nevertheless, the temptation looms for me to take the overhead if it arches slightly on my side, and I am learning to resist and defer to him for the most effective move for us as a team.

I'm learning to defer overheads to Jim, to step aside so that he can execute, to give him the center shots, and encourage him to poach. Truly, it is painful if I don't. As a partner, I aim to give Jim room to lead us on the court, and as his wife to take control within our marriage, to make the final decisions, and to defend us at all possible turns based on his God-given, masculine abilities and instincts.

As the wife, when you defer to your husband, essentially, you allow him to protect you and love you as God intended. Learning to trust your partner's instincts both on and off the court takes time, and there may be a few mishaps along the way. My stubborn heart and desire to take control has gotten me into more messes than I'd care to admit.

Nevertheless, I've discovered the pleasant and comfortable joy of letting Jim lead on the court and at home. He has proven himself worthy of this task. He values my input and opinion, yet when we are at a crossroad, he mans up and makes the decision. Unless there are extreme reservations on my part, we go with his gut.

As Christ followers, the same is true. You concede to your heavenly Father, His Word, His wisdom, His way. When you take the reins and begin to do life your way without deferring to God, expect to fall flat on your face. If you do, rest assured that He will gently lift you, dust you off, and encourage your heart to try to trust Him again even in the smallest ways.

Reflection: In what scenarios do you struggle to defer to God? To your spouse? Why is optimizing your partner's God-given strengths and abilities important on the court and in marriage?

Prayer: Dear Jesus, help us to defer to your will for our lives and marriage. Teach us to trust you more with each passing day. May Your will be done. Amen.

The man who sanctifies his wife understands that this is his divinely ordained responsibility... Is my wife more like Christ because she is married to me? Or is she like Christ in spite of me? Has she shrunk from His likeness because of me? Do I sanctify her or hold her back? Is she a better woman because she is married to me?

—*R. Kent Hughes*

DAY 12: The Pickleball Topspin - A Positive Spin on Life

Finally, brothers and sisters, whatever is true, whatever is noble, whatever is right, whatever is pure, whatever is lovely, whatever is admirable—if anything is excellent or praiseworthy—think about such things. (Philippians 4:8)

In pickleball, adding topspin to your shots adds an upward curve to the ball, giving your team extra power and control of the game, making it more challenging for your opponents to return. Likewise, in your marriage, choosing to focus on the positive aspects of life and dwelling on thoughts that are uplifting and encouraging will bring you positive returns.

A good portion of pickleball players do not take advantage of adding topspin to their game, and the same is true in many marriages when it comes to maintaining a positive outlook in life. Couples tend to accept the humdrum and mundane or they allow those negative, pesky and annoying things about their spouses to dampen their outlook and cause them to feel disgruntled or somewhat pessimistic.

Once when I arrived at the court, a friend said, "Is anybody looking for a husband? You can have mine." Another standing joke from the guys is that all the married couples should line up facing one another. Then on the count of three, every man should take one step to his right, and the woman in front of him will become his official new pickleball partner.

It's so easy to pick our partners apart (after all, their defects are glaring, right?!). Many couples I know, as well as Jim and I, find it easy to treat our spouses way differently than we treat other players. And this ought not to be. Whether you're playing in league or tournament play, you will want to put your best foot forward with your spouse. Nit-picking is divisive and quickly kills your camaraderie.

Once when facing off against opponents that Jim and I most likely should have beaten in a tournament, I put a ball back into play that was clearly flying out of bounds. (And maybe this wasn't the first time that day.)

"Stop hitting balls that are out!" he remarked firmly and with an otherwise exasperated look. Instantly, my heart fell, and I imploded. Although I needed to be mindful of where I was standing on the court, offering me that reminder at that time did me in emotionally. I lost it and began thinking a gamut of defeating thoughts like: *He is frustrated with me! He hates my playing style. He thinks this is a waste of time. He would much rather play with someone else than me.*

I know that's a far jump from reality, but if you're like I am, your thoughts can get the best of you if you're not careful. Stop the toxic thinking in its tracks, and instead choose thoughts that reflect Philippians 4:8. This is where you will find the grace you need on the pickleball court and within your marriage. A united front adds dimension to your game and puts you at a marked advantage before your opponents. They see you as strong and in sync with one another, not squabbling and uncooperative.

Reflection: When is the best time for you and your spouse to discuss sticky issues in pickleball and your marriage? How might you steer your thoughts in a Philippians 4:8 direction?

Prayer: Dear God, help us to fix our minds on positive and praiseworthy thoughts. May we spin our words and actions in uplifting ways, reflecting the goodness and joy that come from following You. Amen.

Great marriages don't happen by luck or by accident.
They are the result of a consistent investment of time,
thoughtfulness, forgiveness, affection, prayer, mutual respect,
and a rock-solid commitment between a husband and a wife.

—*Dave Willis*

DAY 13: The Pickleball Slice - Embrace Uniqueness

There are different kinds of gifts, but the same Spirit distributes them. There are different kinds of service, but the same Lord. There are different kinds of working, but in all of them and in everyone it is the same God at work. (1 Corinthians 12:4-6)

You know who they are. Those players who add incredible spin to their balls, stalling you out or ensuring you will blast the ball right into the net on your side as you attempt to return their slice. Executing or returning a spinning ball can be tricky but is a highly sought after skill in this game, especially for advanced players.

Just as the side spin shot or slice in pickleball adds uniqueness to the game, you and your spouse bring your own gifts and talents to a marriage. Learning to embrace and celebrate your unique characteristics adds spice to your union and offers you a more complete toolbox with which to navigate life.

A healthy mental focus is reminding yourself often that your unique qualities complement each other on the court and in your marriage. Ditch comparing yourself to other marriages, and instead pinpoint the distinctive strengths you each bring to the partnership.

Jim enjoys having fun on the court, whereas I'm much more competitive and put a good deal of emphasis on snagging the win. Jim can be a bit goofy, cracking jokes about fried chicken or telling his opponent to try harder to smack back those shots he sends sailing out of bounds toward them. He laughs a lot and genuinely enjoys the game.

On the other hand, in league or tournament play, I tend to press him sternly to "focus!" Sometimes he looks back at me like I'm a Martian, responding with, "I'm doing my best. Try to have fun, will ya?!" Together, we make a solid balance of fun and competition, but it takes work for each of us to appreciate and applaud our differences.

Adding sidespin or slice to your pickleball shots creates unpredictable angles for your opponents. Similarly, in your marriage, embracing each other's uniqueness adds layers of depth and excitement to your relationship. It's like admiring a vibrant kaleidoscope.

Just as each colorful piece forms a stunning pattern in the kaleidoscope, your individual qualities connect to create an uncommonly beautiful relationship. Celebrate your individuality and recognize that your unique qualities complement and strengthen your partnership on and off the court.

Reflection: In what ways are you and your spouse similar and different? How do you handle the uniqueness you bring to your marriage? Do you feel like your strengths and weaknesses are being managed properly? Why or why not?

Prayer: Dear God, thank you for creating us uniquely and gifting us differently. Help us to appreciate and support each other's strengths, working together as a team in our marriage and on the pickleball court. Amen.

No matter how many rules we make for ourselves,
rules don't create godly relationships.
Only leaning on our faithful Father and longing to
please Him with everything we do will
set the stage for a beautiful romance!

--Eric Ludy

DAY 14: The Pickleball Crosscourt Shot - Priorities

But seek first his kingdom and his righteousness, and all these things will be given to you as well. (Matthew 6:33)

Prioritizing a crosscourt shot in pickleball when you receive your opponent's serve gives you time to rush to and control the net with your partner. A hard crosscourt shot, delivered with power and precision deeply into your opponents' court, keeps them back at the baseline. If you return the ball short or gently loft it back, your team becomes disadvantaged in ways.

As former tennis players, Jim and I both understand the importance of and have prioritized deep returns of serves. Once when playing indoors and fighting a black plastic hanging curtain not five feet behind the service line, he cautioned me that my returns were way too soft and were only teeing up the receiver to blast it back at us. I complained to him that I struggled to get a wind-up to powerfully strike the serves. It felt uncomfortable because I kept hitting the heavy tarp with my paddle. I had to adjust my determination to execute an effective crosscourt shot.

The same is true in marriage. When you and your spouse make it your top priority to seek God first in everything you do, this behavior and attitude allows you to respond powerfully to whatever life may serve your way. It requires determination and intention. Seek Him first through prayer and petition, trusting that this will offer you maximum safety and security. Seek Him through His Word knowing that His timeless wisdom and guidance await you. Seek Him in the morning as you arise and must tackle tasks before you and in the evening as you lay down to rest.

Your "power" in marriage comes from a vibrant, intimate relationship with your Lord and Savior which in turn allows you to behave more intentionally with your spouse. The benefits of spending time with God in Bible study and prayer overflows into your marriage as well as all your relationships.

When your spiritual tank is overflowing, then you can more readily invest time in your marriage, giving it the priority it deserves after God. Playing pickleball together (something fun) helps offset some of the other routine or mundane aspects of your marriage (like managing your home, working, etc.).

Just as you will reap the benefits of prioritizing God in your life individually and as a married couple, remember that playing pickleball together can also be a valuable investment in your marriage and relationship. The sport offers a boost to your physical and emotional health and enhances your overall well-being. You get fresh air, loads of Vitamin D, and get to connect with your friends. Of course, playing pickleball shouldn't consume your life, however, when balanced with your other commitments, it can offer you a fun and easy way to do life with your spouse. God first, then family, then your community and your church, with pickleball thrown in there somewhere in between.

Reflection: What do you and your spouse do to prioritize your relationship first with God, then with each other? Are your priorities balanced according to your values and Biblical principles?

Prayer: Dear Lord, guide us to prioritize our relationship with you above all else. Grant us wisdom in balancing our commitments and responsibilities while keeping our focus on you. Amen.

There is no more lovely, friendly and charming relationship, communion or company than a good marriage.

– *Martin Luther*

DAY 15: The Pickleball Counter Punch - Respond with Grace

Get rid of all bitterness, rage and anger, brawling and slander, along with every form of malice. Be kind and compassionate to one another, forgiving each other, just as in Christ God forgave you. (Ephesians 4:31-32)

The counter punch in pickleball requires a calculated response to your opponent's shot. Likewise, in your marriage, when your spouse takes a verbal jab at you, instead of punching back or reacting with anger, quickly respond with deliberation, grace, and forgiveness, just as Christ forgave us.

It is no secret that your spouse will annoy you at times and vice versa. We all get angry for many reasons, but generally, you'll want to check your anger at the door. When you're feeling miffed or irritated, you may be tempted to scream "Foul!" or to give full verbal vent to your frustration. Maybe you were inconvenienced. Perhaps you felt afraid. It could be pride welling up in your heart, puffing up, and seeing your spouse as your foe not your partner.

Have you ever felt so disgruntled at missing a shot or losing a pickleball game that you've hurled your paddle into the grass or slapped your leg with your paddle so forcefully that others heard or noticed the smack? Although I've not done those things, when I've felt "punched" on the court and lost a game, sometimes it's all I can muster to walk to the net for the polite paddle tap. I barely grumble, "Good game."

Depending on how you respond when pricked a bit, there might be something much deeper boiling in your soul. It could be time to repent and ask God to reveal those anxious thoughts you harbor in your heart and mind, especially when things don't go your way, or you feel bristled. When you get jabbed by your spouse, it's so easy to retaliate with blame, to justify your behavior, or to make excuses instead of calmly addressing the core issues.

When provoked by your spouse on the court or off and for whatever reason, you can choose to respond with kindness and respect. This will help you grow closer as a team and will keep you from majoring in the minors.

Responding with grace in your marriage fosters an atmosphere of love and understanding. Embrace forgiveness and compassion, knowing that responding with grace brings harmony to your relationship.

During a counter punch in pickleball, your response to your opponent's shot requires agility and control. Similarly, in your marriage, responding with grace and forgiveness during conflicts demonstrates emotional intelligence and understanding. Responding with grace brings healing and strengthens your partnership.

Reflection: Are you short-tempered? Do you accept constructive criticism? Is your general heart's attitude one of forgiveness and humility?

Prayer: Heavenly Father, help us to let go of negative emotions and attitudes. Fill us with kindness, compassion, and a heart willing to forgive, reflecting upon the grace we continue to abundantly receive from You. Amen.

Only when marriage and family exist for God's glory and not to serve as replacement idols are we able to truly love and be loved. Remember, neither your child nor your husband (or wife) should be who you worship, but instead who you worship with.

—*Mark Driscoll*

DAY 16: The Pickleball Fake - Honesty and Transparency

Therefore each of you must put off falsehood and speak truthfully to your neighbor, for we are all members of one body. (Ephesians 4:25)

Jim and I have a friend who has mastered what we call the "One-eyed Jack." When he returns a particular type of loft, his head and eyes face one direction, yet, as his paddle swiftly strikes the ball, he sends it in the exact opposite direction. Often his opponents are caught off guard and stand befuddled as the ball bounces past them. I've seen other players who wind up as if to slam the ball, only to gently tap it over the net catching their opponents by surprise. In your marriage, on the other hand, any degree of fake outs with your spouse is unwise and damaging as you both aim to be truthful and transparent with each other, even when it hurts.

Honesty is crucial in marriage for several reasons. As you read through the list below, highlight any reason that seems particularly important to you.

1. Trust: Without honesty, trust cannot be established or maintained. Trust is vital for emotional intimacy, and it allows you to feel secure and supported in your marriage.
2. Communication: Open communication fosters a deeper connection and helps prevent misunderstandings that can lead to conflict.
3. Vulnerability and Authenticity: Being open and truthful about your thoughts, emotions, and experiences creates a safe space where you and your spouse can express yourself without fear of judgment.
4. Problem-Solving: Dishonestly concealing problems instead of trying to address and find solutions to them can lead to unresolved issues, resentment, and long-term damage to your marriage.
5. Maintaining a Strong Foundation: When you choose to be truthful to your spouse, you add a layer of strength to the base of your marriage. This helps you to withstand external pressures and internal challenges.
6. Personal Growth: Sharing your goals, aspirations, and personal challenges without reservation allows your spouse to support you on

your individual journey in life which contributes to a sense of mutual respect, love, and honor.

7. Intimacy: Do you share your deepest thoughts, desires, and fears with your spouse? If so, you help to strengthen the emotional connections you share and create a more fulfilling, satisfying, and intimate marriage.

Sometimes it takes courage to say openly and honestly what you feel. When I need to tell Jim something on the more serious side, I can think of a gazillion reasons why I should just keep the issue to myself. Internally, I say things like: *I don't have time to talk about this. He might feel hurt if I tell him this. He might even be angry. It's not that big of a deal. I'll handle this myself. I already know what he'll say.* The truth is you have a choice to be a 100% fully disclosing spouse or not. Choose wisely.

Reflection: Is there any area of your life that you are keeping hidden from your spouse and/or your heavenly Father? Why? Pray for courage and make time today to share any secrets or toxic thinking that may hinder or damage your relationship.

Prayer: Dear God, help us to have the courage to be honest and transparent with one another. May our communication be marked by truth and trust, not fear and shame. You hate lying lips, yet you graciously forgive. Help us to follow your example and lead. Amen.

The ideal husband understands every word his wife doesn't say.

--Alfred Hitchcock

DAY 17: The Pickleball Ernie - Seizing Opportunities

Be very careful, then, how you live—not as unwise but as wise, making the most of every opportunity, because the days are evil. (Ephesians 5:15-16)

If you've watched pro pickleball for a long time, you've seen the experienced players execute a perfect Ernie by leaping over the kitchen while forcefully smacking the ball out of reach of their opponents and landing with both their feet now out of bounds. The exciting Ernie shot in pickleball requires seizing the right moment to move forward. Similarly, in your marriage, be wise and make the most of every opportunity to love and serve each other, knowing that time is precious.

Sometimes taking advantage of opportunities on and off the court requires taking risks. In pickleball, perhaps you want to try something new like bouncing the ball instead of drop serving it. Maybe you want to try to poach, seize that Ernie moment, or even start serve stacking with your partner. In all cases, choose to embrace a growth mindset, recognizing that taking risks fosters learning and development. Celebrate the courage it takes to seize opportunities, regardless of the outcomes.

Seizing opportunities in your marriage is like catching lightning bugs on a summer night. Just as fireflies appear fleetingly, opportunities for growth and connection may present themselves briefly. Successfully grabbing hold of these moments and making the most of them will strengthen your bond by lighting up your marriage with love and wonder, joy, and gratitude.

I love adventure. As a matter of fact, that is precisely what my mentor and her husband firmly declared to Jim the night they first met him: "You must find ways to keep the passion going, to feed Victoria's craving for adventure."

To this day, Jim has still been trying to figure out how to do this. Recently, I asked him if there was something near illegal, but not illegal, that he could think of that we could do. *Pause.* His surprised eyes turned to a bewildered gaze, and his smile slowly faded into pursed lips the longer he stared at me and realized I was dead serious. *Pause.* "Okay, fine. What about something to get our adrenaline going?"

Surprising me with roses, well, that's nice, but it's not what feeds my soul. Surprising me with a rock-climbing adventure, now that speaks to me. Seizing an opportunity for a quick getaway or a hike through the woods or even a trip to the local mall (like we used to do when we were non-dating) -- these are the actions that speak directly to my heart.

The Ernie shot in pickleball involves an instinctive move to catch your opponents off guard. You must be poised and quick to execute this shot. In your marriage, you can also embrace spontaneity and take advantage of moments to emphasize your affection and attentiveness toward each other.

Reflection: How can you demonstrate your affection and love for your spouse in ways they would most enjoy and find rewarding? What can you do today or this week to seize an opportunity to bless their heart and soul and show them just how much you care for their needs and desires?

Prayer: Dear God, help us to be wise and discerning in our actions. May we deliberately find ways to bless our spouse, making the most of every opportunity to show love, kindness, and grace to each other, recognizing the value of each moment we share. Help us to pull an "Ernie" in our marriage today! Amen.

In God there is no hunger that needs to be filled,
only plenteousness that desires to give.
– C.S. Lewis

DAY 18: The Poach - Stepping up to Take the Load

"And over all these virtues put on love, which binds them all together in perfect unity." (Colossians 3:14)

In pickleball, "poaching" typically refers to a strategy where one player moves laterally across the court to intercept a shot that was intended for their partner. The purpose is to surprise the opponents, take control of the point, and put pressure on the opposing team.

Frankly, I love it when Jim poaches and puts the ball away! It's quite exhilarating and brings me considerable relief especially when our opponents are formidable or of the "banger" variety. By poaching, he intercepts what might have been a hard shot toward me, and I find this move protective and helpful. Too much poaching, however, might really get on my nerves because then I don't feel like a contributing partner holding my own weight, so to speak.

In marriage, effective anticipation is crucial. Just when you are at your wit's end, your spouse can step in for a well needed "poach." They can take the heat and help deflect a few hardships coming your way. Together you can support each other and work collaboratively to address issues or provide assistance sometimes without being explicitly asked.

Life will often send a few hard balls sailing your way. Exercising flexibility in marriage and on the court allows you both to respond effectively to unexpected situations. Further, you can incorporate unexpected gestures of love and appreciation in your marriage which can strengthen your unity and emotional connection. Just like the Ernie shot, you can surprise your spouse with their special dinner or a night out at a movie. Step in and take the lead with a poach.

In both pickleball and marriage, success often comes from being attuned to your partner, communicating effectively, and strategically navigating the dynamic environment. When Jim and I are playing, I try extremely hard to know exactly where he is on the court. I strive to be in sync with his movements and body language.

In our marriage, I aim to notice his countenance, his verbal tone, and general disposition. Some days, he is consumed by his office work at home and needs me to show support by closing his door or keeping the dogs quiet. If he's in the middle of a home project or chore, I ask to see if there's anything I can do to help, and I trust that he will specifically tell me. I bless him by bringing him a cup of coffee or making his lunch. I try to respect and honor where he is and what he's doing every single day. Although Jim's personality is extremely low key, friendly, and approachable, some days he needs his space. I remind myself not to take this personally, but instead to make room for him to be himself. I try to lighten his load.

While the contexts of playing pickleball and being married are vastly different, the principles of teamwork, communication, and adaptability can contribute to success in both areas of your life.

Reflection: How do you feel when your partner poaches in pickleball? What if they miss a shot? What do you do from time to time to help your spouse carry a heavy load?

Prayer: Heavenly Father, bless our marriage with love, mutual support, and effective communication. Help each of us take up the slack when the other feels weary or tired. May we seize moments to surprise the other with thoughtful and meaningful gestures to highlight how we have each other's backs. Amen.

It is not your love that sustains the marriage,
but from now on, the marriage that sustains your love.

--Dietrich Bonhoeffer

DAY 19: Words - Control Is King

Do not let any unwholesome talk come out of your mouths, but only what is helpful for building others up according to their needs, that it may benefit those who listen. (Ephesians 4:29)

The words you use in pickleball with your partner, as well as within your marriage, are critically important because they can impact communication, teamwork, and the overall health of the relationship. The Bible says that your tongue has the power of life and death (Proverbs 18:21). Because you long to speak life over your spouse and partner, gaining control over your tongue is a wise and valuable pursuit.

And this is where I have truly come unraveled. After a few losses with Jim, I find myself wanting to lash out at him verbally and give him a piece of my mind. In my own self-centeredness, I try to find someone to blame for my poor playing or even solid playing but having lost the game, and he's an easy target. Not only this, but sometimes I'm not too kind to myself either.

Words have the power to build up or tear down, and effective communication is essential for understanding and supporting each other. Want to find the root of your issue? Examine your heart! Jesus proclaimed that your mouth speaks words that your heart is full of (Matthew 12:34). Malicious words, maligned heart. Death-filled words, darkened heart.

We've all said things we regret later, and we know firsthand just how hard it is to tame our tongue! Fortunately, we've been forgiven much and can love much in return. Ask God to help you control your words and clean your heart of anything ungodly. Encouraging words, compassionate heart. Life-giving words, heart of Christ.

Compelling sidenote: You might find the definition of the word "profanity" as included in the *USA Pickleball 2023 Official Rulebook* quite interesting: "Words, phrases, or hand gestures, common or uncommon, which are normally considered inappropriate in 'polite company' or around children. Typically included are four-letter words used as expletives or verbal intensifiers" (3.A.27, p. 14). Referees may issue fouls for this type of tongue slip.

If you've let a curse word rip a time or two, challenge yourself to get a bit creative and begin using a new word to let off a bit of steam. One of my friends cries out, "Horse Feathers!" and another "Dagnabbit!" or "Rats!" In all cases, consider those around you with listening ears, and attempt to show self-control for their benefit and to honor God.

Reflection: How would you describe your speech in general? Do you use your words like weapons as constructive, uplifting blessings, that allow those listening to have hope and trust?

Prayer: Lord, we confess the times our tongues have not reflected Your love and grace. Forgive us for the moments when our words have caused harm and pain. Help us gain control over our tongues and fill our speech with kindness, encouragement, and understanding. Help us catch our spouses doing something right and reaffirm them verbally. Amen.

> Determine to pray more words over your marriage
> than you speak about your marriage.
>
> –Lysa TerKeurst

DAY 20: Faults and Forgiveness

Therefore confess your sins to each other and pray for each other so that you may be healed. The prayer of a righteous person is powerful and effective. (James 5:16)

I recently asked Jim what he thought my faults were in our marriage and on the pickleball court. His answers did not surprise me in part because we have discussed them often.

"Victoria, in our marriage you struggle with jealousy and trust. Yet, I see how you recognize this and pray for God to help you overcome these insecurities. You let me know ways that I can better support you and show you just how much I love you and how I have eyes only for you. On the court, especially in high stakes games, you make winning your sole purpose. You hate to lose, and when you lose, you say things you really don't mean." Yep. He nailed it! Faults. We all have them.

In pickleball, faults refer to rule violations that result in the loss of a point or the serving opportunity. The three most common faults in pickleball are foot faults, double-bounce rule violation, and non-volley zone (kitchen) infractions which lead to side-outs or point loss.

Three common "faults" most marriages face include: communication breakdowns, unmet expectations, and lack of intimacy. These faults can lead to misunderstandings, resentment, disappointments, dissatisfactions, tension, emotional distance, and even loneliness. If you're reading this devotional, my guess is that you and your spouse strive for effective communication and compromise, and you are committed to working together to strengthen your relationship both on and off the court.

Although the examples I gave you in my own marriage are ongoing types of issues, I must habitually confess my faults to God and to my spouse, accept forgiveness and grace, and with God's help continue to develop personally and as a team.

So much of pickleball and marriage is a mind game. When I make mistakes, it's easy for me to "get in my head." My thoughts go rogue and lead me to ungodly conclusions. I work hard to "take my thoughts captive" (2 Cor. 10:5) and to "be transformed through the renewing of my mind" (Rom. 12:2).

The key? Forgiveness. A commitment to navigate any challenges you and your spouse face is where beauty unfolds. Confession leads to forgiveness and purification. Whether it's a foot fault or a relationship misstep, the path to growth involves forgiveness of yourself and your spouse, renewal, and a commitment to move forward together.

Reflection: How do you handle it on the court when your partner's toe slips over the kitchen line, and you lose the point? How do you handle it in your marriage when your spouse trips up in some unfavorable fashion? How quickly do you forgive and move on?

Prayer: Lord, forgive us our sins. Help us put on the mind of Christ each day. Teach us to offer forgiveness for mistakes, both others' and our own. Give us hearts that long to be more like You and guide us in this transformation. Thank You for modeling true restoration of our souls by giving us the greatest gift of all: Your Son Jesus Christ as our personal Lord and Savior, the One who died for our sins so that we might live. Amen.

I have held many things in my hands and I have lost them all;
but whatever I have placed in God's hands, that I still possess.

--Martin Luther

DAY 21: The Pickleball Victory - Celebrate Together

But thanks be to God! He gives us the victory through our Lord Jesus Christ. (1 Corinthians 15:57)

Remember that jealousy I struggle with? Sometimes when Jim and I lose together, but then he goes on to play with another woman and wins, well, I'd just as soon eat a bucket of nails as to witness their victory.

I know. It's ugly. And what does God have to say about jealousy? Proverbs 14:30 reads: "A heart at peace gives life to the body, but envy rots the bones." The true and lasting love that I long to have for my husband includes celebrating his personal victories and accomplishments. When he wins, we win. It means I am fist bumping like crazy when he grabs a victory or plays his heart out and loses, no matter his partner. Isn't this what the Lord does for you and me? Our victory is His.

The Bible teaches that you have victory through Christ. Jesus defeated death and you have eternal life if you confess your sins and believe in Him. Do you know Him?

How might you celebrate your victories in life? You can give thanks to God for His blessings, recognizing that every triumph is a result of His goodness. Acknowledging God's role in your marriage and seeking His guidance and wisdom leads to a deeper spiritual connection and a more profound sense of purpose in your relationship. Trust in His plan for your relationship, and know that with God as your divine partner, your marriage is destined for greatness as "a cord of three strands is not quickly broken" (Ecclesiastes 4:12).

Celebrating victories together in your marriage is like raising a championship trophy as a team. Just as snagging a medal at a tournament is the culmination of hard work and unity, celebrating together in your marriage reinforces the joy of shared accomplishments and creates a culture of support and appreciation. Take time to celebrate milestones and achievements, savoring the journey you've traveled together. Celebrate that Christ is at the helm of your marriage and that ultimate victory belongs to Him.

Remember: There will be a day when you will throw all your crowns to the feet of Jesus. Keep fighting the good fight. Run to win this race. And run to win with your spouse right by your side.

Reflection: In what ways do you cultivate a spirit of camaraderie in your marriage and on the court, celebrating each other's achievements as individual or team players? How do your spouse's successes strengthen your marriage?

Prayer: Heavenly Father, help us to focus on the prize far greater than a pickleball medal. May we together celebrate all victories and blessings in our marriage and lives knowing that you have been, are, and will be present with us on this journey and against all opponents and challenges we may face. Thank you for your faithfulness to grow us and develop us as a team on and off the court. May our hearts overflow with gratitude and joy as daily we declare, "Zero, zero, start." Amen.

Many marriages would be better if the husband and the wife clearly understood that they are on the same side.

–Zig Ziglar

MONTHLY MARRIAGE

TUNE-UP QUESTIONS

During one of your regular date nights, grab this list to get the conversation started on the overall health of your marriage and relationship.

1. What am I doing now that you especially enjoy?

2. What's one of your favorite traits of the Spirit that I demonstrate? "But the fruit of the Spirit is love, joy, peace, forbearance, kindness, goodness, faithfulness, gentleness and self-control...." (Galatians 5:22-23a)

3. Are there any household chores or duties you wish I would take over? Are there any you prefer for us to do together?

4. What do you love the most about our sexual relationship? What might you change?

5. Describe our friendship. Are you content with our emotional, physical, and intellectual intimacy? Do you feel challenged in any of these areas? How might I help you to feel happier?

6. On a scale of 1-10, with 10 being the strongest, how connected would you describe our overall level of connectedness?

7. Do you have any areas of insecurity within our marriage? What might I do to help you feel more secure, safe, or protected?

8. Is there anything I've stopped doing that you used to like? Have I started doing something you don't like?

9. Is there anything I do that you'd like me to change? Do you know why this is important to you?

10. What's something specific I can do this week or month to help you feel loved or supported?

11. How have you been hurt recently? Has this issue been resolved? What would offer you the greatest healing?

12. Are there any areas of unforgiveness toward me that you are harboring? Do you find that I am unforgiving in any way toward you?

13. In what ways are you keeping God at the center of your relationship with Him? How are we doing this as a couple?

14. What can I pray for you this week?

15. Are we spending enough time together? Do you need more space for anything?

MARITAL EMOTIONAL "TANK"

Take a few moments monthly to run through this list to make sure you're operating at full throttle. Is there anything you can add?

FILLS UP	DEPLETES
Intimate connection / sex / hugging / touch	Lack of sexual intimacy
Laughter / Smiling / Glad to see someone	Serious faces/expressions
Quality time together	Too much time away – too busy
Problem solving	Too much focus on family issues, "drama"
Meaningful conversations/discussions	Arguments / contention / unresolved or non-addressed issues
Adventure / Spontaneity	Feelings of boredom or humdrum
Shared interests and excitement	Not much personal cross over of interests
Setting goals together in all areas of life/marriage	Just drifting without a plan or aspirations
Words of encouragement / affirmations; Loving, Thoughtful words	Nit-picking and criticism, complaints, and seeing the negative more than the positive
Showing appreciation, Loving Thoughtful Acts	Taking advantage of the other
Privacy – just the 2 of us notions or team mentality / Shared secrets and inside jokes	Publicly sharing intimate details or accounts, poking fun of the other, putting the other down publicly

Daily prayer and devotion together	Not praying together or sharing spiritual blessings
Active pastimes together (walks, pickleball, etc.)	Each going own way so to speak, pursuing own interests at expense of marital union
Eating together / enjoying meals	Eating apart / each on their own
Going to bed together often at same time	Disjointed on night routine / no "pillow talk"
Having pet names or silly habits	Not connecting in childlike ways
Texting to stay connected when away	Texting friends and others more often
Communication courtesy and priority: Saying I love you often, etc.	Forgetting to say "I love you" or "Good night" or including each other in day-to-day of it all
Phone priority: Answering phone calls and texts in timely way – special ring tone, override, etc.	Staying on phone with someone else or not stopping conversations when spouse calls or walks in room, etc.
Feeling special, giving unique attention in social settings; being the first to know things	Giving others extended attention, speaking one-on-one with the same gender is isolated setting; someone else telling you something about your spouse that you didn't know

ABOUT THE AUTHOR

As a devotional writer for *Guideposts Strength & Grace* magazine, certified Christian life coach, host of the Choose 2 Think inspirational podcast, director & educator at Choose 2 Think Academy, YouTuber, Christian motivational speaker at women's retreats and conferences, as well as a university Spanish instructor for nearly 30 years, Victoria inspires others to find God-honoring happiness through her signature and transformative method for mind renewal: *The 7 R's for Living Your Best Thought Life.*

Victoria has written Bible studies, taught Sunday School, led and spoken at small women's groups, authored books, and blogged for years. Her writing has also been featured in *Just Between Us*, a world-renowned Christian magazine. She's the proud mother to four children and four grandchildren, and she and her husband Jim live in Lexington, Kentucky, and playing pickleball is always on the calendar along with hiking and traveling.

CONNECT WITH VICTORIA

Website: www.choose2think.co (yes, that is *.co*)

Find information here about **mentoring and online courses.** *Be sure to subscribe to the* **Choose 2 Think bi-monthly newsletter** *to stay in touch regularly.*

Email: choose2think@gmail.com

Inspirational Podcast: Search "Choose 2 Think" anywhere you listen to podcasts

YouTube: Choose 2 Think Inspirational Podcast @choose2thinkpodcast

Facebook: Choose 2 Think Inspirational Podcast Community

Instagram: Victoria D. Lydon

Pinterest: Choose 2 Think

To get your FREE RESOURCE to accompany this devotional, Visit *www.choose2think.co and click PICKLEBALL FREEBIE*

www.ingramcontent.com/pod-product-compliance
Lightning Source LLC
Chambersburg PA
CBHW062126040426
42337CB00044B/4330